THE LITTLE UNLUCKY LEPRECHAUN

A Tale of Believing in Oneself Beyond Luck

BY JACQUELINE DUREN
Illustrated by Kim Gorrasi

The Little Unlucky Leprechaun
Copyright © 1996 by Jacqueline LaFlamme

Illustrations Copyright © 1996 Kim Gorrasi Studio
All rights reserved. printed in the U.S.A.

This book may be purchased in bulk for
promotional, business or educational use.

Library of Congress Catologing-in-Publication Data is available.
ISBN: 978-0-578-39550-0 (paperback)
ISBN: 978-0-578-86032-9 (hardback)

Book design by Jacqueline Duren

First edition, 2021

The illustrations in this book were created with
watercolor and gouache on canvas.

For Capri & Sienna.
May you always believe in yourself
beyond any token big or small.
Your heart will always lead you
where you need to be.
I love you more than you know.

Mom, without your light and love I would not be who I am today. Thank you for believing in me more than I could some days and pushing me toward my best self.

ONCE UPON A TIME, there was a little leprechaun who was no bigger than a pinky finger. People say leprechauns are lucky, but this little leprechaun was not.

He was terribly unlucky...

He would daily get lost when playing in the grass. In school he didn't have many friends and getting good grades was difficult for him too.

Everyone in Leprechaun Valley would laugh and giggle at the little leprechaun, calling him names and teasing him.

The little leprechaun's misfortune would cause him to cry after school until he couldn't cry anymore.

UNTIL SOMETHING MAGICAL HAPPENED...

WALKING HOME FROM SCHOOL HE FOUND SOMETHING MAGICAL.

When walking home from school in Leprechaun Valley he came across a patch of clovers. In the middle of the patch there was a small four-leafed clover. He picked it from the patch and took it home.

It was after that moment that the little leprechaun's luck turned around.

Could a clover bring luck?

The little leprechaun truly believed that the clover could bring him luck.

He brought his new lucky clover everywhere he went.

He brought it to school, and got good grades. He brought it to the park and made new friends. He also brought it into his backyard and he never got lost in the grass!

Days passed and the little leprechaun was happy and joyful all the time.

A FEW WEEKS LATER...

The little leprechaun lost his clover. "Oh no!" he cried. He didn't know what to do!

He thought and thought and cried all night.

The little leprechaun decided not to tell anyone because he didn't want to be laughed at by all in Leprechaun Valley.

The next day, he pretended he still had his clover.

He went to school, and got good grades. He went to the park and met new friends. He even went for a walk in his backyard and didn't get lost.

This went on for weeks, but after these weeks passed, he stopped thinking about his lucky clover.

Now I know where luck comes from.

The little leprechaun said to himself. "Well, I don't have my clover, and I am still joyful and happy." Luck comes from your heart not a clover.

If I believe in myself, I can be the luckiest leprechaun around! From that day on, everything was just as it should be.

The little leprechaun loved and believed in himself and knew that he could do whatever he set his heart on.

grew up in Massachusetts love for writing. The Little was written for her school the book to encourage all young children to believe in themselves when she found trouble doing so for herself at a younger age. Since then, Jacqueline has remembered the message from

JACQUELINE DUREN

The Little Unlucky Leprechaun and carried it with her through some of life's biggest challenges. For readers young and old, Jacqueline hopes everyone believes in themselves a little more after reading this book and shares the message of courage, compassion, and love with others. Her interest in reading, writing, and telling stories led her to a career in communications. She is the mother to two beautiful little girls and wife to her biggest fan.

About the Illustrator

Trained in Florence, New York, and Boston, Kim Gorrasi has achieved success as an illustrator, gallery artist, and portraitist. Gorrasi has illustrated for *M. Grumbacher, Inc., The McGraw-Hill Companies*, and *The Cricket Magazine Group*. She has exhibited in galleries across the U.S. Her portrait commissions reside in the collections of *Harvard University, Bentley University,* and *The Players Club of New York*.

CPSIA information can be obtained
at www.ICGtesting.com
Printed in the USA
LVHW061342260422
717122LV00009B/439